GW00750212

Black Wolf on a White Plain

Mary Montague

Sally
September 07.

SUMMER PALACE PRESS

First published in 2001 by

Summer Palace Press
Cladnageeragh, Kilbeg, Kilcar, County Donegal, Ireland

Printed by Nicholson & Bass Ltd.

A catalogue record for this book is available
from the British Library

ISBN   0   9535912   5   5

for
Ann Breslin

Acknowledgments

Some of the poems in this book have previously appeared in:

Beyond the Rubicon (Covehill Press 1999); *Cyphers; Fingerpost; Fortnight; My Native Donegal* (Rathmullan Enterprise Group); *Poetry Ireland Review; TickleAce.*

Some poems have been broadcast on BBC Radio Foyle and on Channel 9.

I wish to thank Thornhill College, Derry, for the career break that allowed completion of the manuscript.

Biographical Note
Mary Montague was born in Enniskillen in 1964 and reared in Ederney, County Fermanagh. After graduating from Queen's University, Belfast, she worked in London and Dublin. She teaches in Derry City, and lives in Park, County Derry. She is a member of the Errigal Writers, a cross-border group based in Letterkenny, County Donegal.

CONTENTS

Cabot Trail

Grey is the colour of Cape Breton forests:
green-grey are the flattened arms of the canopy;
dough-grey are the dessicated spruce corpses;
mauve-grey dulls the skin of the blueberry.

Bone-grey, the girlish silver birches
whose moose-torn bark is strewn as pages
on the midden below. Unhidden flesh
burns labial-purple, tan, fawn, pink, peach.

Around the wounds, frayed ribbons peel like gift-wrap
to fringe central stele, woodpecker-pocked.
Over all surfaces – branch, trunk and rock –
cupric-green lichen furzes its slow creep.

Other species, shades of oxide-grey,
spread mottling haloes over dinosaur
eggs that have petrified where they lie
on a dead-leaf salad, brittle as straw.

When the suspended gauze of seeping drizzle
condenses its chill, almost corporeal
it beads the frail cobweb mesh
and mists the blank eyes of lakes.

The dank moss plush is miniature taiga
smothering Mi'Kmaq memory, hushed in saga.
The smell is of fungal decay, mulch and mint.
Growth is slow transpiration, quiet assent.

The Massive Leap

No matter what jumps out at me
ever again, it'll never match
the humpback rearing up from the sea
behind the headland at Beautiful Cove,
as we were stumbling down the stony path
in the almost-dark, having already spent
nearly two hours, breathless, watching
her tail flukes loop out of the water –
that slow glide topped by a fractional
pause, then a push back down
through the slick obsidian surface –
but this, this was an unbelievable
answer to my prayer: *one more
time, please, one more time,*
and that monstrous leviathan
breached with a gushing crash
right over that jut of land
her house-sized, sculled head
volcanoeing up, and her eye, I swear,
seemed fixed on us, as if
keeping track. Nothing
will ever match that.

Pleasant Bay

We stopped at Pleasant Bay –
a perfect name, for the day
was Aegean. We turned our backs,
exhausted, on the breaching pods
of highlands that we'd driven
through, and sat out to sip beer
under a covered deck
overlooking the Atlantic.
The glare was factor thirty plus,
so shade and drink were more
the welcome. As we rested
we noticed, further out,
the slick loping of a school of cetaceans.
What are they? we asked our waitress.
Pilots, she told us, and squinting,
we could faintly see the sonar bulge
of their boffin heads. Sunlight
glanced smoothly off brow, nape, rump.
Being too full, we left binoculars
lying on the table, just raised mugs
to continue sipping, let eyes
fall aimlessly
on the darning of waves
as whales fed past.

Lakeside Epiphany

What is there to say
when you find yourself
lost in the woods in Cape North
and you arrive at a large pool,
screeded by spruce, where moose
come to bathe and cool themselves?
It is early August; the sun
has the height of noon; the sky's
blue tent is an enclosure
into which you've intruded.
You – your strange shape and colour,
your synthetic smell and awkwardness –
your presence has been noted,
but you are let stay.

The first moose
is a brown boulder.
She stands shank-deep
in water, swizzling
her bearded, bulbous head
to suck up weeds and wetness.
She has ears that stick out like a goat's.
Her fur is donkey-brown.
Her withers have the slope
of pyramids. Her ribs are sprung
with the strength of the vault's rafters.
She shows you what an unhumaned,
unharmed world was, and would be, like.
You feel helplessly happy.
She goes on feeding and drinking,
dunking her camel's nose,
snuffling and snorting.
You go on watching.
Your guts are raddled with joy.

Another female, vast,
giraffe-legged, strides primeval
out of the forest and into the shallows;
her head jerks as she notices you
and you think you see
her shoulder hunch defensively
as she wades away
to the far side of the lake;
but she doesn't leave – her sister
gives her confidence and she too
is now slopping through the water,
the hock of one hind leg carefully
raised like the elbow of a harp.
Have you ever
seen such gawky
tender grace as this?

Now a younger one,
maybe a yearling, appears,
cautious, in the reeds.
It's not clear whether this reticence
is due to you or to her elders.
She rolls a nervous eye but also
enters the water up to her belly.
The first moose has moved over,
has turned side-on to you, keeps
raising her head to stare into the trees.
This is unsettling; you watch with her,
wondering what is skulking
where it can't be seen. You feel
fellow-herbivore with your companions.
But it's another moose! No –
it's two, madonna and child,
she stepping gratefully into the water,
her calf, well-grown but with a teddy-bear's
scruffy fawn and dun coat, hesitating
behind. It goes only fetlock-deep
before stopping to nod impatiently
after its mother. Then it turns and stumbles
onto the stony shore to flicker
in and out of the skirting scrub.
Its mother is unperturbed, ploughs on
through the water, a pontoon on stilts.

By now the sun has slipped
a little lower; the lake silvers as glare
softens and colours deepen.
Two greater yellowlegs spiral
out of the sky to land near your feet.
You are astonished to see them –
to find that the moose and you
are not the only living creatures
left on Earth. You see insects
sparkling and remember that some
are mosquitoes, that you'll feel their bites
tomorrow; but your eyes are filled
by the first moose, who has made
her way round to your shore.
Her legs plunge through the water
as she wades out as far as her knees.
She shakes herself like a dog, the showering
drops swarming from her like a scattering
mesh. You see her ever more plainly,
the rough soil of her runnelled fur,
the huge, holy hulk of her. Your advocate,
who asks nothing, is needless of you,
but your need of her, or those like her,
is both ache in your belly and source
of serenity. The lure of her gaze
is almost enough for you to follow
the air disturbed by her passing
as now, finally, she steps
out of the water,
vanishes into the trees.

Curious Girl

After leaping across the road
in front of our car
the white-tailed deer
did not vanish into the trees.
Instead she stopped in the long grass
and turned to stare, just as we did.
Her honeyed neck
grew gazelle-like and her eyes swelled
which lent extra elegance
to the supple line of her throat
and more nectar-sweetness
to the lambent solace of her gaze.
The fluted bells of her ears
stood perpendicular to her lean
and lovely face that twitched
in an effort to fathom us. She
peered with meerkat-craning
until her nerve failed – then
she fled into the shade.

Whycocomagh

We were seated at the window
in the dining room of our inn
near Whycocomagh when I noticed
movement further out in the dusk.
The room was bright, purring
with conversation – some of us
burbling with delight at the baubled
hummingbirds that froze a few seconds,
as they sipped at plastic feeders stuck
to the glass. The movement I saw
was different – not the startling flits
and stops of those insect-like birds
but a rolling saunter across the lawn.
This animal was as big as a large
dog, but its gait was an even tread –
not the trot of a dog – it was the stalk
of a cat. The paws were massive.
The shoulders rollicked with pendular
rhythm, the paddles of scapulae
fluidly jutting in turn, up
through the tawny hide with each
deliberate stride. He – it could only
be he, arrogant as hell, with that
pumped-up androgenic insouciance
of youth – had a ludicrously short
tail and the furry jowls and tufted
ears I knew from childhood reading.

A lynx, a lynx, I squealed. A pause,
then pandemonium as chairs scraped back
and people stood, or scrambled for cameras.
We all stared out at the yellow stage
thrown by windowlight, across which
wildness was passing. The beast himself
was barely interrupted by our commotion.
His head veered a little towards us, the sneer
in his eyes hardening to that of a mogul's,
but he swaggered on with the same cadence
to emphasise his derision. Yet no time
elapsed until the curtain of trees parted
then closed behind him. Inside we returned
to our incongruous food, jabbering
excitedly like a mob reassuring
itself as danger drifts on.

Sitting Bull

My glance snagged on the irregular
imprint outlined against cabbaged
vegetation beneath the spiked trees.
I peered disbelieving at what seemed
to be massive plastic antlers
placed judiciously low to the ground.
My breath stalled as I saw the attached
head with its heavy lumpen brow
and unfazed eyes that flung back
my stare from under the craggy
head-dress of reclining majesty.

A prime bull moose! My stomach bucked
at the sight and my body seemed
poor package to his asserting bulk.
The Miocene was recalled by heaped droppings
and huge footprints incarnating their maker
downwind at midday. To disturb him at siesta
was to surely risk that rack, those hooves,
but he didn't move, just held my gaze.

Minutes passed. My stiff legs complained.
I didn't want to shift, wanted
to remain in this mutual
surveillance but something
had to break. I almost
moved on, almost had the maturity
to let the moment live in memory.
Instead I tried to trap it.

Extricating my camera, I felt
sacrilegious as its zip snarled
the silence but when I looked again I found
I was still favoured by his regard.

I snapped three or four times. The sound
and flash brought further fixity of stare
but no apparent fear. As I waited,
spirit thrilled at the primeval contemplation
but flesh now itched for movement:
even in the face of this immensity,
detachment threatened. I roused my brain
for a farewell scrutiny to inlay
the details: the humus-brown fur and geeky
ears; his bovine solemnity; the blank visor
of his face that was crowned by lobed
concave platters cresting like a laurel
wreath above his broad pate.

Now I could creep off along
the rough-cobbled mud-slimed
path and congratulate myself
on my ability to let him go;

but the path veered, threaded closer:
a gap opened; there he was,
the nearest wild ungulate
I'd ever see. A base urge
swept through me – *take him, take him!*

I snapped twice more. The first flash
caught him square in the eye.
Hindquarters soared alarmingly
as he staggered to his feet.
Standing at his full frightening
height, he was worth it –
worth any keratin-smash
just to see this, this close.

Then the second flash confirmed for him
his unwisdom and, to my relief, he shambled
off, the dromedary hump of his withers
a fulcrum for the diagonal shift
of his shoulders. His backward eye
watched me until the forest enclosed him.
How could such a giant move so quickly,
erase himself so delicately? I was left
adrenalin-jittered, staring
into the hollow where he'd lain.

My First Experience of Beauty

My first experience of beauty
was when I was four years old
on the strand at Rossnowlagh
on one of those days that becomes
a legend of childhood.
The sky was an intense blue,
unscummed by cloud,
the sea offered itself up
with jewelled certitude.
Suddenly there appeared,
on the sheer cliffs overhead,
three horses who shone
with youth, health and sun.
Later I would learn the given
names of their gleaming hides:
bright bay, dark bay, chestnut.
Then, all I could do was squint up,
determined to absorb them:
the barrels of their solid bodies
above lean and delicate legs
that were shortened by the height
and angle; the skeins of swishing
tails that flounced against each other's
interloping heads, which hung,
with the curiosity of the young,
to stare down at us. I fell back
on the sand, its grit fanning
underneath the splay of my shoulderblades,
to tell myself, also for the first time,
Remember this, remember this.

The Silent Pianist

I hear her
telling me of how she cried
to learn the piano.
There was no piano
at home, no money
for lessons, but her longing
was a contorting need
that pleaded and pleaded.
Somehow enough was scraped together
to send her, aged seven, to the convent
to Mother Joseph of the fierce passion
and fiercer ruler, who bore down
on my mother's enthusiasm
and pressed her into musicianship.
My mother remembers
the easing, the slightest show of pleasure
on the nun's tight face
when this thin, fair child
showed signs of promise, patience
and practice. At home
that girl practised on the kitchen
table; she pummelled
the silent surface into a whispering
pulse of pattering sound.
Her numbered fingers pranced, paraded,
paused as music sang out
in her head. Her feet worked
invisible pedals, her eyes closed
as her hands fluttered, lifting
and falling with the same fragile
determination as a butterfly in flight.

Sally

in memory of Ida

Everybody's being especially kind to Sally.
Eyes clouded, she wanders about,
suddenly all of her eleven years,
the sparkle gone, her romping
vanquished by her mother's vanishing.
Never again will my eyes be pleasured
by looking down on those two
golden collie backs treading lightly
in tandem, a smooth unity
of grace and gentleness
as I walked them up Howth Road.

Dreamtime

After school the darkening fields called
to me and I'd struggle to cross them.
With little of the day I could claim
for myself, I clung to this instinctual
marking of territory in the face
of winter glooming. My dog would sweep
ahead and his regular, tongue-lolling
glance was my only encouragement.
I prided myself that I knew these fields
better than those who owned them.
In that season there were few to challenge me,
certainly not the desultory bullocks
who could distil themselves from the murky
air to glower at us with deep, apprehensive
eyes. The ground was heavy and wet, each
rush-tufted clod demanding attentive
placing of feet; even my familiar
crossing-points in those barbed hedgerows
required respectful negotiation,
so I'd suspend my horse-persona
until I'd clambered through. Then
I'd resurrect my delicate hooves
and wind-lifted tail, feel the arch
of my neck and swivelling ears, and I'd
roll my eyes and dilate my nostrils
at shadows in the dusk – never mind
that my scalp itched under my woollen
cap and that I could hear little except
the heaving punctuation of my breath.
When frost came to harden this hummocky
turf, I'd gallop over it at will.

As the drumlin's curve descended
and the laser-tunnels of headlights
swept along the road below, I'd start
the fall of the parabola
that would bring me home. Once, just past this apex,
something flared in the hedgerow beside me,
something small and dull but with a tawny flag
that caught the last warmth from the greying sun.
A spool of fluff with a beady eye,
a twitch of indignation – a robin
on the hoop of a bramble that spilled
from the skirts of the hedge. He fixed me
with his glare as he danced a stilted
warning not my own body's length away.
His pouting chest, ruffled forehead and flipped-up tail
blasted his incongruous aggression.
I was frozen by his passion.
Only seeping chillness would have prodded me on
but my dog came blustering back
with ears pricked to inquire what was keeping me.
The robin skimmed away into the dusk. I called
my dog and crouched beside him to stroke
his shaggy length while he slobbered
and thrashed. When I'd touched him enough,
I stood up, real again, able
to make my way home in the dark.

Meanderings

One strolling summer Sunday we set out
through the wooded hills above the Suir
valley. We were three cousins who met only
during the annual family gathering,
so we had little for conversation,
but Cathy had had the sense to bring
with her a radio and this soothed our
lulls with the afternoon charts. We swayed
along in loose floral skirts, the cotton
stroking our bare calves, coaxing our latent
ease in the blossom of our bodies,
us not yet fourteen and mistrustful
of the unbidden power nestling inside us.
The gravelly path was bright with sunshine.
Sweat sprang up to check our pace when we pushed
too hard past drowsy lassitude.
As the incline levelled, the trees bunched thicker
and we swam with relief into the cool pools
netted by their shade. I felt a lapping
thrill at our undulating saunter,
the possibility of confidence,
benevolence. If we could idle
through the woods like this,
maybe the rest was negotiable.

My cousins have long left the liminal
state I hold to. I've returned alone
to retrace our steps on another sultry
afternoon. My feet crunch the path, my gaze
calms to the sweep of this river valley.
I plod on, uncertain, to the rhythms
of twenty years ago. I no longer
pause on every threshold but some reticence
has stayed through wastrel years, has stood me
at the edge so long it seems to be
the only place I fit in. As my mind
eddies, loops back, the river flows on.

Betrayal

You were taken underwing
by the calls of *biddy, biddy, biddy,*
as the frantic chickens scuttled
to devour the scattering.

You were soothed by the murmur
of *suck, suck, suck,* as doe-eyed calves
rattled their meal-buckets or raised
glistening muzzles for a quizzical gaze.

You revelled in the charge
of tramping the hills to check the sheep,
or collecting the cows for milking.
In their trust you were at peace.

The comfort of kitchen conversation
of which you were a part,
where it all came together
in strong tea, wheaten bread and hearth.

But the whimpers that were sometimes heard
from a hidden, unmentioned coop emerged
one morning as two collies, famished, craven.
Their innocent error was to be untrained.

To sheep and fowl they were a threat
and the effort to make them benefit
wasn't thought worth it. You saw with horror
the brutal limits of the farm's nurture.

The Shepherdess

In Mayo
my car almost collided
with the outrunners
of a flock of sheep
coming over a rise.
Their shepherd followed –
a boy in his mid-teens,
glaring red hair,
dappled copper skin – a lean
epitome of Irishness, loping
to contain the panicked insurrection.
His eyes flicked to mine,
chin inflecting acknowledgement.
Struggling behind
came his sister, another
Irish cliche, but paler,
fatter, slower. I was shocked
at how obviously adolescence
was ravaging her: her awkward
determined dignity; the mortifying
bounce of her breasts; her turned-away
face. She passed me,
eyes stuck to the ground.
It was several seconds
before I could leave her,
floundering in the wake
of her brother's leadership.

Intrusion

She was standing out on the road. I couldn't
pass that unassailable request. She gathered
herself into the car with the careful gestures
of a clucking hen. I took in her slight body,
short grey hair and disconcertingly fresh face.
She started chatting as I slid the stick back
into gear and while I drove, that bright and brittle
noise kept us company. It turned out, of course,
that she knew my father, knew of me so she asked
all the questions that had me mortified
as a teenager. When we reached the village,
despite her protests, I drove on through, out
the back road and then took a turn I didn't know
not three miles from my home. *You've never been on*
this road? Make a wish then! and as my thoughts
flitted to the future, she said it for me:
For a good man! raising her hands delightedly.

It wasn't for that, I grinned, glad of the truth of it.

Ah, I suppose all the men are the same, says you.

Ach, I wouldn't say that either.

                    Aye, well,
the young men seem to be different; they seem
to treat their wives better.

And as we crawled through the leafy twists
of that narrow road in the mild sunshine of autumn
I wondered what pain she'd lived out, here in seclusion.

Round the next bend, she told me, *but you can turn
here*, indicating a gateway.
                                    Not at all,
I overrode her and swept her, clamouring,
to a scruffy hedge, a glimpse of grey stone,
a litter of debris, a dark silence.
                                    Thank you,
thank you – her voice screeched at me.

                                            I turned
in the sucking laneway and drove off ashamed
of my self-serving magnanimity
and my patronising feminism that trod
on her grace, brushed aside her sensitivity.
I had left her exposed and feeling shabby
with only promises of prayers
and remembrances at Mass to barter with.

Accidental Death

When it came
it was as casual
as an unthinking caress,
as automatic
as smoothing a strand of hair
behind the ear –
an instantaneous snuffing
as avoidable
as stepping on the cracks
of an even pavement.
She was dead
before she could see
what hurtled towards her,
bruises arrested
pre-bloom, as her blood froze
leaving her yellowed
and husk-like.

We blundered about in her wake,
bludgeoned by the fact
and its lack
of meaning. Her life
which had seemed boundless
now halted
too soon, too abruptly for any to bear.
We fell back
in confusion on *Hail Mary*
and our enchanting prayers for the dead;
met each other
with lucent eyes and nodded

at those who stammered
of God's greater plan while their voices
petered out with grief.
How to explain
Death, the inexplicable, in this extremity?
Youth, beauty, talent – no protection.
We stand around the chasm,
skinless
in the face of random cruelty,
knowing
the bower of reality,
breakable
as bone.

The Young Fulmars

The young fulmars
are wheeling through the air,
swirling and sweeling
as they circle the cliff,
sailing the updraft on stiff wings.
Their dolphin-grey feet trail out like pennants,
their tubular nostrils perch like pince-nez
on the bridge of their beaks.
They have a severe and military eye,
and the awkward, dexterous grace
of a Sopwith.
When they swoon up
to the near-empty ledges
their shoulders hinge slightly
and their wings shiver to shed air
as their tails flare and cup
the backdraft, make of it
a column, a hub, a pole
to grip and slow themselves
so they drop with a lubberly plop
onto the clods that purchase
a rest, a nest place
around this giddy bowl.
The adults, the others,
are all gone. It is autumn.
The season is over, but
these youngsters remain,
practising, practising, practising
for spring.

Atlantic

Breakers gush geyser-high,
and splash down over rocks
to leave them mane-rivuleted
as the sea gathers
itself for another storm
past vestigial sharkstooth shards
whose token stance
provokes joyous venom
from the deriding waves.
On they chunder
to where the land
hunkers down, offers a shoulder.
Water bunches, shoves
between legs of rock, jumps
pockets and spouts a final
flinging embrace.
This giddy flourish of spray
flags a surrender to chaos
that rides a fierce and passionate rhythm.
Who's to say that if the tides were not
dragged and dizzied by the moon,
the hungering swell
would not still be drawn down,
sucked in, to the somnolent hulk
of land which knows itself blessed
by this primordial pulse,
this ancient roar.

Learmount November

Tawny corridors of beech
have shed a mat of battered
bronzeleaf onto the trails.
The frail larches have faded
to pale gold. The air
has the clean dampness
of freshly washed hair
and the wind has failed
to disarray all the shawls
of leaves which drip their hues:
wine; rose; copper; greenfinch-yellow.
Seedlitter – chestnut and beech –
cobbles the ground. Wet-slate
trunks sprawl since the storms
of two winters ago. Downhill
the Faughan has burgeoned
and, at one curve, has collapsed
the bank into a pit of debris.
A sycamore has been wrenched
out from the roots and is prostrate
in the water. On a shelf of rubble
a white disc flashes to show
the drop-winged curtseys
of a dipper. It brazens
a few seconds, then slips
into the otter-slick river
to meld with the rushing brown.

Sighted

A buzzard pendulating,
its swooping interlocking
of wing with wind
waltzing it back and forth
as it lowers its undercarriage
to slow its heavily
deft twist in the air.

If that's not enough,
on the way down the mountain
a splurge of goldfinches
bursts from the hedge
dousing the view.

December's Close

The story of the night
is written in the snow.
The paths of the forest
are necklaced with foxprints.
Rosaries of pads record
the patrols: the long famished
strides with the furrow
of tail-tip white-lining
the snowcrust. There must
be scores of foxes in these woods:
tracks parallel and weave,
scissor across, edge up to clumps
to snuffle all chances.
The night was long with several
snowfalls to freshen each alien
coating. A single success is marked
where the surface is bloodied
and scuffed, the prints circle
and scatter. Further on,
a scraping where the kill
was set down for the captor
to gobble and gulp. No fur
or feathers remain, just
a frozen nugget of flesh,
a nail-white square of fat.
One victim enough to fortress
a warm mammalian body
against the petrifying air,
enough to get through
another bitter night
of cold and snow and death.

The Pheasant

That birds are
the direct descendants
of dinosaurs I have no doubt

as my car slams
to a stop at the sight
of a male pheasant
stalking the road,

his fixed eye glaring
in his vivid lizard-green
head which bobs reptilian
over the scaly patterns
of his neat body.

He turns away,
nervous but supercilious,
the hocks of his huge
hind legs arrowing up
to his long tapering tail,
and squeezes through the fence

leaving me
to marvel
at this little
cousin of the allosaurus
scooting across the grass
between the legs of cattle
in a Donegal field.

Disturbance

I am waiting
for the noise to start.
My whole body
is an enormous ear,
a taut membrane
stretched to grimacing tension.
At last
the racket erupts
to xylophone my vertebrae,
frazzle my stomach,
tighten my jaws,
resound in my chest.
I am filled with noise, noise, noise.
My brain sizzles. I want
to wail, to roar, to bawl with grief;
but I am paralysed,
impotent.
There is nothing I can do to stop this.
I can't even prevent
my own predatoriness
as I crouch, ready to pounce
on the first faint stirrings.
Like a scavenging stoat
I swivel to their source.
I am undeflectable. I have
become a saucered receiver
waiting to scream as bombs rain down.
A transformer:
sound vibrates me
to a furnaced throb.

Salvaged

I'm finished
with being witness
to your distress.
This is no lack
of tenderness
but rather
weariness
of being the catalyst
for your despair
and the punishment
for your errors.
Neither salve
nor salvation
lie with me
and only driven desperation
forces this brutality.
I'll not be your all-consuming:
for me another life is waiting.

The Land

I never saw the land in daylight
but when I left him home the car moaned
up a high and slippery track, sheep scuttled away
and I could see the bleak and boggy plains
with rush clumps and still dark pools
which enclosing sky veiled with mizzling rain.
Even high skies were grey and patterned by wind
that only in summer might blow all away,
leaving a serene blue backdrop for the flowers
and insects that rose out of the coarse grass.
But such astonishing days were too little sustenance
over months of struggle when only hands were blue,
then white, as fingers grappled with handles and
gates and baling twine, and daylight was a rush
from field to yard to outhouse and back,
to check, to count, to feed, to mend, before
damp and dark drove you inside to the fire and
there was damn little money and even less satisfaction.

Except times, on a half-good day,
when you could stand on the hill
or lean on a gate, and know that though
they dwarfed you, yet you'd marked them:
that the shape of them was formed by rock
and soil and rain, yet it was you who
held it as it was, who decided that this
should be drained and nourished, and now
shone jewel-bright against its mossy neighbours,
and that should be let lie; that those trees
should be planted here to shelter this, and
those lambs should be moved here at this time,

and back again at that; that we should switch
from hay to silage now, and to do that
we should buy this and build that, and do this
and wait for that. All of it showed:
your routine and risk, your judgement and method,
your invention and pattern – and it worked.
You were still here; you could still stand on this ground,
black and bitter stuff, and say, I've played my part,
even as it fell away from you, in its own inevitable rhythm.
You were bound to it, shaped by it,
as fiercely as it was by you.

The imperative of the land had given
self-possession in bondage,
self-reliance in necessity,
strength in simplicity,
and this I mourned
even as I admired.
I knew I'd never fit myself to it.

Cloves
for Kate and Joan

One sniff
and I inhale
all the sweet stench
of smoky pubs, the huddle
of winter, diffusing warmth
of hot ports and whiskey,
glue of conversation and
the grinning disintegration
of our separate selves
into one benevolent glow.

Trespass

The retrovirus
injects its blueprint
for replication
and death.
The foreign chain
of nucleotides
co-opts the cell's
own machinery
in order to re-constitute
its message
as DNA, copied
for special effect
on the body's own defenders.

These fifth columnists
harbour a secret
that spurns lysis,
to let them slide into position.
Insinuated in the host
chromosome, apparently
acquiescent to containment
within this larger life, the parasite
is a trigger cocked, waiting
for the signal that will loose it
to destroy the lymphocytes.
The finite human body
is left as feast
for hordes of passing microbes
which mulch it to a teeming,
squalid mass. Trespass becomes plunder.
The phage, unzipped, erects a carcase.

Quest for Quagga

Reinhold Rau *ist* gaga.
He wants to reconstitute the quagga –
that stripeless zebra whose extinction
will thus be granted dispensation
from the finality of forever.

Project Quagga is simply asinine,
a conservational waste of time;
the equine with the unspeakable name
will not be seen in the Karoo again,
for all science's redemptive paradigm.

Head of a zebra, hide of an onager,
a relatively unremarkable herbivore;
occupying the same niche as the American buffalo,
it suffered the same fate, only worse:
butchered to oblivion under the colonists' curse.

That was the genocide of the 1870s,
to be redeemed by genetics in the 1990s.
Mitochondrial DNA substantiates the theory
that *Equus quagga* is a subspecies, merely,
of the common African equid, *E. burchelli*.

No matter that Burchell's, the plains zebra,
is as black and white as the brute fact of death;
as brute as the futile remains captured by camera,
held in museums – ephemera we'll never recover.
We'll never confront resurrection's shibboleth.

But Reinhold's the boy, he's rounded some up –
brownish Burchell's – dictated how they'll breed.
Eventually we'll get a quagga, he's decreed.
That it's been allowed before doesn't help, of course:
the Tarpan, Przewalski's, each the true wild horse.

Extinction's irrefutable, they're not recreatable –
quaggas, thylacines, other obscurities
unbeloved of our children's stories –
vanished, unknown, unremembered.
Being emblematic doesn't prevent it.
Sentimental indulgences won't restore it.

To quest the quagga is just prevaricating;
the Sixth Wave is still accelerating.

Alone

In uncontainable vastness,
in the blackness of no
position or orientation,
there is a procession
of planets out
from a single star.

One throws back
astonishing colour
into the solar stare,
as it turns
from darkness
into light,
an unnerving spin
that reveals
the shuddering skin
of a cyanobacterium.

Unwitnessed, this maintains
its light-transforming revolution
until time, the only explicable
direction, allows men
on another dusty surface,
by standing outside, to internalise
the wonder-terror of our isolation.

Michael Collins

The other Michael Collins stayed on board,
alone, in orbit, while Neil and Buzz
went down to get their glory. There are
no fuzzy black-and-white pictures of him.
I would be pissed off. There you are,
taking the same risks, going through
the same terror and trauma and you
barely make it into the history books.
Where's the satisfaction in that? You
miss the small step, and so the giant leap,
because you're the designated driver?
What is this, a taxi service?
I want to moonwalk too!
Reinstate Mike Collins! That's what I say!
Sure, nobody would have got home without him.

Grounded – *and considerate of John Glenn*

You'd think that once
was enough to be rocketed
out of complacency, once
was enough to be fired out
into the relentless dark with
no promise of return.

                    Maybe

his mind can only deal with
the simplicity of absolutes –
rotations, orbits, measurable
immensities matching his own
overriding imperative of *have
to do it, have to do it.*

                    Maybe

he just couldn't endure the
inevitable mundanities of dis-
traction, confusion, corruption.

But you can't fault his timing:

first –
in his fructifying forties,
peak of his intellectual powers,
just past his prime of physical prowess

and now –
at seventy-seven, a second go,
having spent the intervening years
glaring, sun-like, at his goal.

When
he finally does it,

he'll go out like a light.

Natural Resources

While shepherds watch
their flocks by night
in Transylvania,
a lone she-wolf
wearing a radio-collar
limps economically
across railway lines
and waste ground
disguised
as a large dog.
She makes her way,
evading researchers
with infra-red and telemetric
detection systems,
to the huddling creatures
guarded by mastiffs
and their short-tempered stockmen.
She has only moments
to contemplate herbivores
before being deflected by barking.
She returns
to the city's edge
to scour the rubbish bins.

The Black Wolf

Even at this distance
staring across the gulf of change
thoughts of the Black Wolf still haunt me:

the black and jagged rim of pines
skirts the gleaming snowplain
that stretches out to hunger and oblivion,
under a blue-black dome
shot through with the glint
of fascist stars – entourage
of the moon's blatant suspension;

my attention is tapered
by the sudden appearance
of a small black form
delicately blotting
the vast whiteness,
is riveted by the patient
waverless progress
as across an empty page,
and becomes wonder
at where she came from,
shelterless out of snow.
As she approaches
I remain focused
on a figure dark,
distilled from the air's sharpness,
as the ether of breath wraiths
the brutal outlining of flesh
in this winter desert's glare.

Up close she's all wolf, the grinning mouth
hotly gasping, a measure of her labour.
Snow-grimed feet break the crust,
the pads splayed in useless effort
to spread her weight enough
to carry her freely
over the cruelly softened terrain.
Every step is a yielding crush,
a shortening of leg and gait,
a careful lift of foreleg to gash
the hampering smoothness again.
Dense black fur bulks
the spareness of her body,
the stretch of back, hollow
of abdomen, rack
of ribs. Unquenched inside,
she exults in the scour
of her own breath,
the surge driven by her heart
and the relentless triumph
of determined muscle
mocking her environment,
to push her on and on and on.

Now I watch her move off
as far as ever from the trees
still without sustenance,
and I'm startled to consciousness
as I recognise
that refusal to succumb
to the numbness of the frozen
veldt, that willingness
to live chilling bleakness,
no-other-creatureness
as a black wolf
on a white plain.

Even at this distance
and despite time's surrender of self,
thoughts of the Black Wolf still haunt me.

Hillestad Child

I dreamt I had a Norwegian daughter
who came as cleanly out of my body
as an oiled gourd. She lay ready-wrapped
in crisp cotton, her fledgling face closed
as a white pillow's, her mouth as sulkily
serious as that of an intent cat. I gazed
at her, this foreign thing, safely swaddled
in the awning of this upstairs room.
Then we were below and Margrethe
and Torleif stared hard at me and asked:
What do you want? I was twenty-one,
with troubles enough, so I said: *Give
her to someone who'll look after her.*

I turned over with the thought of her
at fourteen, having grown up in a land
of winter dark, sheaves of sharp trees
and fading soothes of snow. Her voice
would sound to me the musical staccato
of that Nordic tongue I don't understand.
I'd swing past the yearly shock of her birthday,
think of her only as a pale figure moving
like a legend round the edges of memory.
If we were to meet, I couldn't even greet her
with her name, and what would she call me:
*a poor excuse for a woman, to abandon
a child and remain barren?* I drifted
from that silky morning, with its bubble
of false promise, grateful that the wherefores
of my decisions are safe with me,
will not be offered for her perusal.

26 August 1979

I have seen many
foxes since and some
before but none has
stayed like this one.

Today, 26 October 2000,
I hunt out my teenage
five-year-diary with the red
cover and frail lock; with
parallel tracks of the same
day for each year. I read
the summer entries. It had to be
the summer – we were staying
in the caravan. I find it
in my fifteenth year
with a folded piece of paper
sellotaped below the allotted space.

I still had my dog. He and I
went walking every day.
That day we went to Tullan,
deep into the dunes.
We disturbed a sleeping fox.
My dog chased the fox.
I chased them both. The fox
outran us. That was all.

Except
for those lines
and what they now show me.
There is nothing for that date
but the description of the encounter
and musings on it.

I go straight in, no context, no preamble:

> *Frisky froze ahead*
> *of me, ears pricked, tail uplifted.*

> *Immediately I knew*
> *that this was more than a passing fancy.*

I describe how the fox
was curled in the hollow
of a dune, its nose tucked
under its brush; how Frisky
crept on and, to stall him,
I whispered his name

and woke the fox.

It did not see us at first;
it blinked and licked its lips.
Then I write:
> *it looked full*
> *at us and was gone.*

I describe it as *pure lightning;*
how it ran up the high dune,
Frisky at its haunches; how
by the time I made it over the rise
they were both on to the next sandy
cliff, but that the fox had now outstripped
the dog by, I estimated:

        75 yards over a distance of about 400.

I tell of how my dog
        did not appear
        for quite a while
        despite my calls and whistles.

When he did
        he was panting and bright eyed.
        I marvelled again at how I had
        been so close to a sleeping
        fox and the instant reflexes
        of that beautiful animal.

I still feel that marvelling.

The entry hypothesises on how
a fox came to be sleeping out
in the open in the middle
of the day. It postulates
that the fox was:
        an inexperienced, unalert cub;

though against that:
        he was not much smaller than Frisky.

I quote David Stephen quoting a record
of a gamekeeper who stalked a sleeping
fox and caught it by the brush.

I justify the length and exclusiveness
of the entry because:

> *it left an impact on me …*
> *and also because it was the closest*
> *I have ever been to a wild fox.*

That is still true.

Finally, I flatter myself
by lamenting the fatal whisper
that prevented me
copying the gamekeeper.

I close the diary.
I feel as rich as the memory.
It is twenty-one years ago.
The dog, the fox are long
dead; but I am back, back
for the fox, back for the girl,

back for the poet.